W9-BZR-509

A Thousand Paths to a Peaceful Life

A Thousand Paths to a
peaceful life

David Baird

MQP

Contents

Introduction

Why, given everything that we, humankind, have going for us, does it seem so impossible to live out a peaceful life here on earth? Instead, we feel compelled to live life at top speed, to burn at our brightest, day in and day out. In this stress-filled world we have created, our life choices are leading us more toward an early burnout than a long, satisfying, and fulfilling life.

But what if we could change all that? What if life is not, as it often seems, out of our control and in the hands of fate and circumstance, but our very own, to fashion according to our own needs and to live exactly as we feel is right? In this book, with thoughts and voices ancient and new as our guides, we will attempt to claim back control, find an escape route from stress, and learn to lead a truly peaceful life.

Letting Go

Think of desire as fire—a little will warm, too much will burn.

One simply cannot be first in everything.

We must learn not to spoil those things we have with our overwhelming desire for those things we don't have.

Consider life as a sequence of cause and effect, and never rely upon luck.

Do not waste an entire life in the pursuit of a few golden moments.

An armed individual
is invariably tempted
to try his strength.

Time is yours for the taking.
Take your peaceful share of time.

Our ears hear and our eyes see.
What then does our mind do?

**We must not throw away precious
time by lusting after things.**

Our first teacher is our own heart.

**A single disturbed thought creates
ten thousand distractions.**

Only a fool will burn his bed to catch a flea.

**Get a reputation as an early riser
and you can stay in bed until noon.**

It is never wise to allow
your goat to become
your gardener.

Instinct is stronger
than upbringing.

Give neither counsel nor salt until you are asked for it.

A throne is only a decorated bench.

A hungry person is an angry person.

A friend's eye is a good mirror.

Luck seeks
       its person.

Your life is yours for the living—meet life peacefully with a smile.

A peaceful life will never last if spent only in peaceful contemplation of the past.

Be full of life.
Full of energy.
Full of vivid
aspiration.

There can be no
peace while our every
waking thought is
preoccupied with the
belief that we must
live a profitable life.

Sometimes, the answers are in the tones of waterfalls.

Peace is its own echo.

Those who have lived a peaceful life have little fear of death and can meet it calmly.

Gaining experience is rarely a peaceful experience.

One does not create a new life simply by trying to forget the old life. A peaceful life takes new spirit, new values.

Mankind is not naturally a peaceful soul—we spend our lives driven to possess things and then worry about losing them once we have them.

Most will go through life not knowing the limits of their abilities.

Ask

What am I running away from?

Ask

What am I shutting my eyes to?

What is
my beauty,
my pain,
my evil,
my strength,
and my joy?

The majority of
mankind is passive.
We simply lie down
and let things
happen to us.

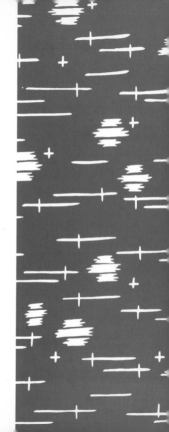

Accept life for what it actually is, a challenge.

For some the achievement of a single day's work will last for eternity.

Fight only for what is right and fair, and give help to those who need it.

Recognize that there is no higher pleasure than that of surmounting difficulties.

Above all,
trust yourself.

We must not build our emotional life on the weaknesses of others.

We must ask ourself if
we are the kind of self
that we will be happy to
live with all our life.

Interest your heart in everything and your life will be filled with adventures.

Forethought wins.

If we fear what lies in the path, we will never move forward.

Much of life is spent fearing what was never there in the first place.

We cannot lead a peaceful life until we learn to bear life's ills rather than allow ourselves to be overcome by them.

Adversity is the frost of life—impressive in its moment and gone with a little warmth.

Let go of the cliff, die completely, and then come back to life—after that you cannot ever be deceived.

Zen saying

30

If everyone is born a king, why do so many opt to die in exile?

Most of the shadows of this life are caused by standing in one's own sunshine.

Ralph Waldo Emerson

**Many a life is wasted
by being too sensitive.**

A little bit of
worry each day
adds up to years
over a lifetime.

This life is for you.

A peaceful life is ours
when we find work
that we love to do.

Many a life is spent just earning a living.

The secret of a peaceful life is not just doing what you like, but to like what it is that you are doing.

Each day treat everything as though you are seeing it for the very first time.

Between the wish and the thing life lies waiting.

A moment spent trying to do too many things is a moment lost.

Plan to
be no less
than you are
capable of
being.

**We don't have to be the
best, only to do our best.**

There is enough tragedy in the world—why intentionally bring more into your own life?

The happiness we pass to others is happiness we gain.

We gain strength from the temptation that we resist.

**Do the right deed, and
do it for the right reason.**

Live with intent.

We must learn
who we are and the
things we can do.

We must learn to accept that
we cannot always do those
things that we would like to do.

Natural ability without education has more often raised a man to glory and virtue than education without natural ability.

Cicero

Sometimes at the crossroads of a decision it is helpful to know that others have traveled this way before.

A long way through
the journey of life
we start to learn the
limits of our abilities.

**We can show what
we are capable of
through our work.**

Never start what you do not understand.

Never leave undone that which you can do.

Why is it that we wish to do what we see others doing, even if we would not do it well ourselves?

If you think you can do something, then do it with all your heart. Belief is the key.

Never tell a child that something is impossible, for that child might surprise you.

Those with good fortune do not necessarily have good sense.

You may go through your entire life feeling incompetent but you cannot live by incompetence alone.

When we learn to tackle problems with what is within our power to do, then we stand a chance of success.

Mankind has the ability to elevate his life by his endeavors.

God isn't interested in our ability, only our availability.

They are able because they think they are able.

Abilities are something we all have in common.

The thing that makes us different from others is how we use our abilities.

When you arrive at a peaceful life nothing can draw you back.

Too much zeal spoils everything.

Our freedom to pick and choose is laced with difficulty.

The ultimate path is without difficulty.

There is an old Zen saying that compares Zen to gold and dung: Before you understand it, it's like gold; once you understand it, it's like dung.

Strength of belief is to be admired only if those displaying it can also show the grounds of their belief.

Don't allow your exuberance to block out the light needed for your journey. Knowledge is the light— exuberance without knowledge is a journey in darkness.

We should view youth as a quality we all have, not treat it as something that circumstance has taken from us.

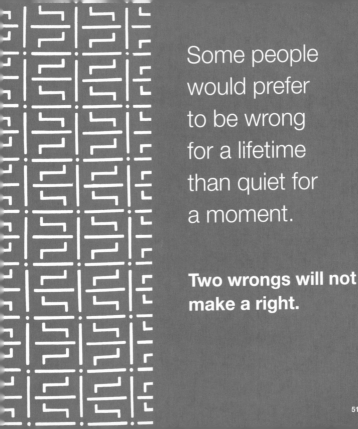

Some people
would prefer
to be wrong
for a lifetime
than quiet for
a moment.

**Two wrongs will not
make a right.**

Curiously, those who cannot endure being in the wrong are most frequently the ones who are.

As Mark Twain said;
Never do wrong when people are looking.

Far better to suffer wrong than to do it.

Which is preferable?
To accept that we will be sometimes cheated or to go through an entire lifetime not trusting at all?

Those who have some belief
appear to cross over from
this life more peacefully than
those with no belief at all.

**It is ludicrous to go through life in
search of peace believing that we
are only able to find it in death.**

Find your stillness in the peace
of wild things.

**Do not tax your life with
forethought of grief.**

Find peace in the presence of
still water.

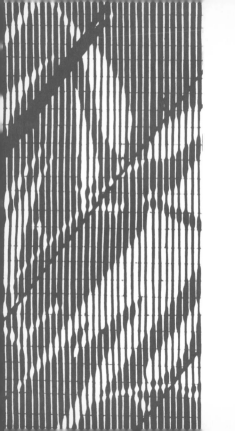

Often
patience
achieves
far more
than
force.

It's not just you—everyone feels down occasionally.

Feeling discouraged is perfectly normal.

Even sadness can be a friend sometimes.

Each and every human being
has passing moods of
dissatisfaction with life.
It is the human condition.

**At times of loss, grief is the
best release.**

Anxiety and panic disrupt the
lives of many.

Recognize the symptoms of your anxiety and get to know the root causes.

Certain fearful thoughts may quickly trigger anxiety or panic.

An unpeaceful life is filled with reminders of anxious times.

Take action today and begin
to experience the peace and
hope that life has to offer you.

Read books.

Any time is a
wonderful time to
begin anything at all.

We are all striving for a peaceful life but some of us work three times as hard and try to buy it with our sweat and blood.

Some of us are so determined to live that we're ready to die for it.

We will never know who our
true friends are until we call
out in times of adversity.

**Those that hold us down stay
down themselves.**

Never let evil see evil. Therein
destruction lies.

We must learn to find the peace that lies in each dark and tragic moment.

Everything can change in a moment.

Excess
Baggage

There was never yet
a philosopher
That could endure
the toothache
patiently.
William Shakespeare

Surround yourself with positive influences, whether in the form of people, inspirational music, or writings.

There are no bad ships, only bad captains.

All work and no play is not good for productivity or a state of well-being. Find time to talk with your workmates—try and find common ground outside of work.

Don't make
mountains out
of molehills—
a lost shoe,
a misplaced ticket,
or a common cold.

Accept it for what
it is, without panic,
and move on
in life.

When a person grows up
surrounded by ridicule, they
learn to be shy.

When work is a pleasure, life is joy!
When work is a duty, life is slavery.
Maxim Gorky

Try not to make impossible
demands on others—
or yourself.

Tackle boredom by finding new ways to do everyday things.

Put some money in a box each time you do something that you would rather not do. When the box is full, treat yourself!

Keep difficult situations in proportion.

Through zeal, knowledge is gotten; through lack of zeal, knowledge is lost.

Buddha

Are you expecting to please everyone?

When disaster strikes, ask yourself, "Am I over-reacting?"

Why do we feel that we must prevail in every situation?

Adopt moderate views and see stress as something that can be coped with, then it can never overwhelm you.

We are all too quick to put down others. Let's change all that—try and note one positive thing about each of the people you come into contact with daily.

For one to win, another must lose.

Never lose your sense of perspective. It is your most valuable weapon in the fight against stress.

When a person grows up surrounded by encouragement, they learn confidence.

Stress breeds stress;
it is a vicious circle.

**Do not betray the trust of
those who have faith in you.**

Have I been true to my word?

Have I practiced
what I taught?

Know in your mind that all
things change.

When a person grows up
surrounded by praise,
they learn to appreciate.

Learn to separate
the wheat from
the chaff.

Always speak the truth and be charitable in speaking to others.

Do not kill the hopes and dreams of others—or yourself.

When a person grows up surrounded by fairness, they learn justice.

Do not steal time.

Do not lie,
especially
to yourself.

**Avoid alcohol and drugs;
the peace they bring is false.**

Practice restraint.

Try to choose an occupation that promotes peace or uplifts humanity, rather than those which increase confusion within humanity.

Dwell upon distinctions and you will find it impossible to live in peace and harmony.

When a person grows up surrounded by security, they learn to have faith.

Confusion often manifests itself in hatred; it cannot be overcome by more hatred.

A man's life consisteth not in the abundance of the things which he possesseth.

Those who keep the physical pleasures in perspective will live in peace and harmony.

Those who are truthful in their encounters with others will live in peace and harmony.

Ask about your neighbors, then buy the house.

As rain penetrates an improperly shingled roof, so passion overwhelms a confused mind.

If a man is destined to drown, he will drown even in a spoonful of water.

The mouth invents what the eye cannot see.

It is not good to be always alone, even in paradise.

No amount of sugar can sweeten a bitter heart.

Do not put yourself in the way of temptation.

None of us are happy with our looks, so we do something about them.
Perhaps more of us should be less happy with our minds.

LIVE—if only to satisfy your curiosity.

Ability is sexless.

Christabel Pankhurst

Distrust those who exalt
unrighteous peace as better
than righteous war.

Those who are capable of oppressing the weak are not capable of living a peaceful life.

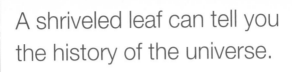
A shriveled leaf can tell you
the history of the universe.

**When a person grows
up surrounded by
approval, they learn to
like themselves.**

We are worthy of all when
we have given up all.

Every moment is a challenge
to our equanimity.

Life is like a movie,
the screen is blank—
we must project
upon it.

Give up lust and hate; only
then will you arrive.

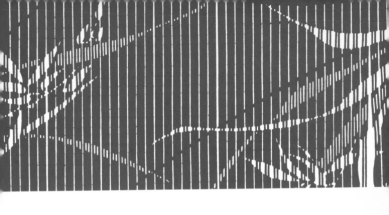

Our reflection in
the mirror only
looks at us because
we look at it.

We can choose whether to be another brick in the wall or a window.

That which you grasp is that which you are.

Cut yourself off from selfishness, doubt, lust, and hatred.

The gate that leads to damnation is wide, the road is clear, and many choose to travel it.

But how narrow is the gate that leads to life, how rough the road, and how few there are who find it.

Matthew 7:13–14

Meditate.

Do not meditate on the pleasures of the senses.

Those who meditate are on the path to harmony and a peaceful life.

Meditation is the source of wisdom.

Enjoy the company of others who live peaceful lives.

Self-examination will help achieve peace and harmony in life.

Guard against destructive thoughts and negativity.

Peace is fragile.

Calm your mind and center yourself in the oneness of infinity.

We are our own masters and protectors and must discipline ourselves accordingly.

Cut off the stream of craving.

Conquer desire.

Every moment is
a golden one
for him who has
the vision to
recognize it
as such.

Henry Miller

All earthly manifestations of infinity, including ourselves, will disintegrate back into infinity.

Those who live peaceful lives are beacons of light, and serve as inspirations to us all.

Too many are motivated by the desire to harm others in order to satisfy their own ambitions.

A peaceful life will not be
gained by hurting others
through words, thoughts,
or deeds.

Violence is always a negative force.

What is the value of finely tailored clothing if the soul is ragged?

No great intellectual thing was ever done by great effort.

John Ruskin

Being born into a noble family, or possessing wealth, or holding a respected title, does not guarantee a peaceful life.

Throw off the chains of confusion.

Tell yourself that you are not one
who is confused in fear.

**Tell yourself that you are not one
who is confused in attachments.**

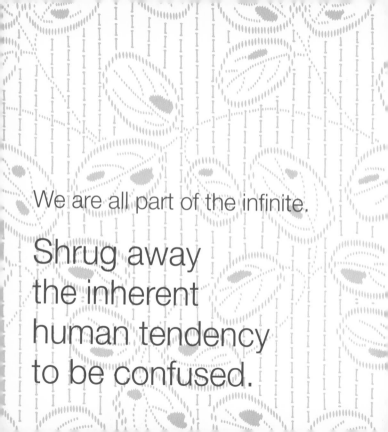

We are all part of the infinite.

Shrug away
the inherent
human tendency
to be confused.

Remain innocent but endure.

Remain centered and you will be able to bear any punishment, abuse, or blame that is laid upon you.

Remain disciplined in body, mind, and speech.

Remain dutiful even when tempted by anger or passion.

Do not cling to
transient pleasure.

Anxiety is a burden—
cast it aside.

Be aware of past and future lives, but do not dwell on them.

The shallow-rooted tree is threatened by even the gentlest breeze.

Strive to live in harmony with the environment and society.

All God
wants of
man is a
peaceful
heart.

Meister Eckhart

A little of what you like does you good—indulge yourself.

You'll never see the good if you cannot endure the bad.

It is no use cultivating a calm and dignified exterior if inwardly you are confused.

Difficult situations are
not disasters.

There is no peace, saith the Lord, unto the wicked.

Isaiah 48:22

The big thieves hang the little ones.

It is not healthy to go through life believing that it is safer to be feared than loved.

Slow down—
you cannot shoe
a running horse.

Smile.
Why not? Try it in at least one encounter a day and gradually build on it. Watch the results in yourself and others.

Beware—truth can make enemies.

A good word is a
good word whether
written in blood,
ink, or pencil.

**Not everybody knows,
but some will try.**

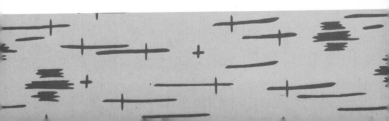

If you set an example by being correct, who would dare remain incorrect?

Confucius

New opinions are always suspected and often opposed just because they are not yet common knowledge.

Never assume that which is incapable of proof.

Everything is the concern of all.

Death is nothing to fear.
It is only the uncertainty of
not knowing when or where
we go that frightens us.
All this changes when we
consider ourselves part of
something infinite.

You cannot be an atheist if you half believe in a God.

Choose everything as you would choose a friend.

Be patient and tough; someday this pain will be useful to you.

If you have nothing, what do you fear losing?

Sometimes the greatest moments can arrive on a donkey.

Avoid giving needless offense.

Strive to be an inspiration to yourself and to others.

We are only
willing to live
if we are
willing to learn.

If you can spend
a perfectly
useless afternoon
in a perfectly
useless manner,
you have learned
how to live.

Lin Yutang

Priorities

Do not allow the acts of others to frighten you and their acts will fail.

You can pull the teeth from the wolf but its inclinations will remain.

If you can find as much pleasure in losing as you do in winning, every moment will be filled with possibilities.

Heaven offers you a soul.
Earth offers you a grave.

Don't ask the spoon the flavor of the soup.

Learn what it is you love.

Every cloud has a silver lining.

Deal with the faults of others as gently as you would with your own.

What man limps because another is hurt?

Death pays all debts.

Don't throw out the baby with the bathwater.

Show me what you love, and I'll show you what you are.

Only seek the respect of those that you respect.

Travel light.

A learned fool does not know the taste of wisdom.

Instinct is stronger than upbringing.

Live with wolves, and you will learn to howl.

Better a lock than suspicion.

A good denial is the
best point in law.

**A courtyard common to all
will be swept by none.**

Who thinks their
baby ugly?

A thief believes that
everybody steals.

Life is a bridge.
Cross over it,
but best build
no house on it.

**Look not where you fell,
but where you slipped.**

It is better to exist
unknown to the law.

**Does the lean man
understand the well-fed?**

A poor beauty will find more
lovers than husbands.

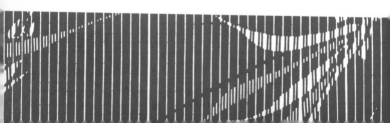

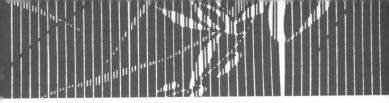

It's not a miracle,
I just decided to do it.

We are all living on borrowed time.

More time, more satisfaction—
it's within us all, and it was
there all the time.

The quality of each moment is far more important than merely getting things done; once we accept this we'll achieve all that has to be achieved with less stress.

All things are a manifestation of our thoughts.

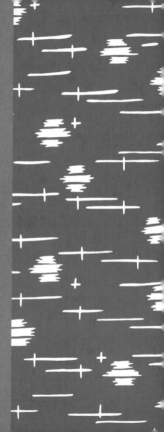

**If one's thoughts are confused,
then one becomes lost.**

Leave the single earthly path and know
that there are infinite paths to follow at
any time, at any place.

**Rejoice in your conquest over
venomous desires.**

Moment to moment, it is difficult to be
a human being.

Respect the peace of others, as you would have them respect your peace.

Be tolerant among those who are intolerant—they are confused.

Be non-violent among those who are violent—they are confused.

Allow your confusion, passion, hatred, pride, and insincerity to leave you.

Words can be the most damaging weapon—guard your tongue.

Never take what is not given.

Do not allow yourself to become confused through desire or attachment to anything.

To an ant a puddle is an ocean.

If you keep camels, make sure you have a big enough door.

Greed
shows us
the fruits,
but not
the tree.

**To a
sightless
man a ruby
and a
pebble are
one.**

The mud of one country is the medicine of another.

If an army of sheep was led by a lion, it would defeat an army of lions led by a sheep.

Never stand in a place of danger trusting only in miracles.

The easiest person to fool
is yourself.

**Examine what is said,
not him who speaks.**

**An inch of time is an inch of gold,
but once lost, you can't buy that
inch of time with an inch of gold.**

Never cut that which can be untied.

The reverse side also has a reverse side.

Commit a sin twice and it will not seem a crime.

If a man is great, even his dog will wear a proud look.

There is plenty of sound in an empty barrel.

Be a light eater, and that doesn't mean start eating the moment it gets light.

**A stylish taunt will repay
a thousand insults.**

We don't necessarily have to
agree with everything we say.

Always have a dream.

If an idea is good, it doesn't
need any help from words.

Once you are dead,
you are made for life.
Jimi Hendrix

An ocean of ennui is enough to drown anyone.

Which is better, dying for a cause you believe in or living for it?

We may have our differences but so long as we are honest, then we are making progress.

One can only be made to feel inferior by giving one's consent.

Speak from
the heart.
It's risky.
It's unrehearsed.
It's spontaneous.
But it's honest.

Nothing is as burdensome
as a secret.

French proverb

Do only one thing at a time.
Simply tackle one problem and
concentrate all efforts on what you
are doing at the moment.

**Nothing can be made simpler if it
is made as simple as possible.**

Call something impossible and someone will spend a lifetime trying to do it.

**Consider mankind—
each human being
mass-produced by
unskilled labor.**

Learn your limits.

The point of philosophy is to start with something so simple as not to seem worth stating, and to end with something so paradoxical that no one will believe it.

Bertrand Russell

There is nothing to be gained from distorting the facts unless you get them straight in the first place.

Those who travel through life like sheep should watch out for the mint sauce.

Our eagerness to gain praise is like a ring in the nose of a bull and leads us away from peaceful living.

Trying to discover why one doesn't have a peaceful life is like staying awake to see if you snore.

Learn to moderate your physical reactions to stress.

Mix leisure with work. Take breaks and get away when you can.

Ruin and remedy are often confused.
Aesop

Get enough sleep.

Strive to develop mutually
supportive relationships.

Set your own goals.

Expect some frustrations, failures, and sorrows.

Learn to relax; by doing so you will be taking control of your life.

Think of thought as a ship on the ocean—it must be navigated if it is to arrive safely.

Take time to learn from nature, it can teach us so many things about life.

Decide to seek a peaceful life and you are halfway there.

A book is like a garden carried in the pocket.

Arabian proverb

**Life is not just a
series of tasks to
get done.**

Life is not just
a series of
meetings we
must attend.

**Life is not just about
accomplishments.**

Never hurry.

Leave
something out
of tomorrow—
the day will be
full enough as
it is.

Looking busy and appearing to be important will not ultimately make you happy.

Make time to get together with friends, with family, with loved ones.

Relax—it is O.K. to feel happy.

No matter what you have, no matter how full your life might seem, if you harbor one iota of emptiness then you will not find peace.

We tend to try to rectify our shortfalls by taking on even more and by working even harder. This will only make us feel more inadequate.

Stop thinking that relaxed people are that way because they work less hard than you or because they are less important than you are.

We are all too busy trying to impress each other intellectually.

The path to a peaceful life is so simple to travel, yet many choose not to understand it.

Resist the temptation to analyze everything that is said to you. It is possible to think too much.

When our conditioned or trained beliefs and responses are challenged one after the other, we have to allow our confusion to be replaced by fascination.

One can view the world as
never-ending conflict, or learn
to be fascinated by the
diversity of human interaction.

Adopt a
positive attitude.

**Don't dwell on time,
it is a race you can never win.**

The secret of enjoying life is learning to live in the moment.

Life is made up of a series of long and short moments.

Don't think yourself into an early grave.

Compare the future with this moment now.

This very moment is precious. Let your mind be here with you in this moment.

Is your thinking taking you to the past? To the future? Or are you right here in the moment?

Our first encounter with peaceful life is when we consciously decide to be in the moment.

Relax, this is your now.

While you plan for tomorrow and fret about yesterday, don't forget to live today.

Simple things are sometimes the most difficult to comprehend.

Unlearn your stress.

You alone are responsible for the quality of peace in your life.

Possessions won't help you to achieve a peaceful life.

It's hope that kills you.

Nothing is cheap
without reason,
nor dear without
value.

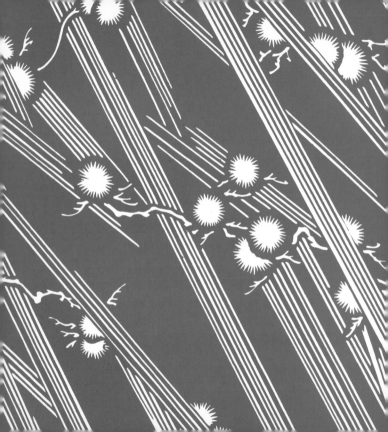

Peaceful
Words

Even a fool, when he holdeth his peace, is counted wise: and he that shutteth his lips is esteemed a man of understanding.

Proverbs 17:28

A man should live
if only to satisfy
his curiosity.

Listen to the music of nature and how it
is composed. Is the song of the whale
so different from our own?

Learn that nothing
is new.

Do nothing secretly; for Time sees and hears all things, and discloses all.

Sophocles

Civility costs us nothing, yet it buys everything.

When you can't shut out the world, watch two birds sitting. Which will fly away first? And when it happens, consider why.

If everybody decided to stay indoors today except one, that person would feel alone and neglected too.

We are never
more alone
than when
surrounded
by a crowd.

**When we build, let
us think that we
build for ever.**

John Ruskin

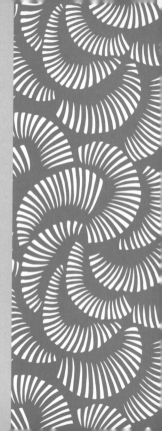

Think of
architecture
as music
frozen in
time.

**Think of graves
as monuments.**

After the first death,
there is no other.

Dylan Thomas

**We all may agree that
something is distressing,
and yet we all will
respond differently.**

When we feel we are experiencing the symptoms of stress, it is a sign that we have gone beyond our optimal stress level.

The only way to reduce stress is to learn to manage it.

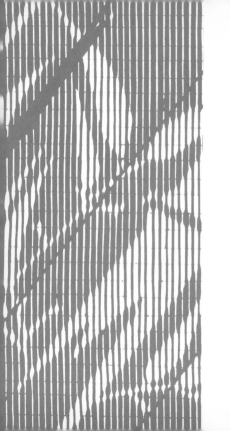

If life was
a book,
it would
make no
sense
at all.

Some thrive under stable conditions and will find varied routines stressful, and vice versa.

Stress begets stress; step back and take a deep breath.

Why should we place more concern on how we look to other people than the way we like to look to ourselves?

I have lost friends, some by death, others by sheer inability to cross the street.

Virginia Woolf

Apathy is the death of the soul.

'Tis not hard, I think, for men so old as we to keep the peace.

William Shakespeare

Set your heart on what it is you know to be important.

An empty vessel makes most noise.

Familiarize yourself with how you respond to stress—perhaps you become nervous or upset?

Learn to know what causes you distress. If you can understand the meaning of such moments, you can learn to manage them better.

It's not just you that has to change. If a red wall at home distresses you, paint it a more peaceful color.

Sleep is sweet to the laboring man.

Shorten your exposure to what causes you stress and find peace in a break from routine or location.

Devote yourself to making a change and set yourself goals that you can achieve.

A high percentage of the turmoil in our lives is brought about by overreaction.

Learn through practice to bring your heart rate and respiration back to neutral. Slow, deep breathing will help.

Use relaxation techniques to help reduce tension.

It is always beneficial to build your physical and mental reserves.

Remember, you can't move mountains except by one stone at a time. Always keep in mind your limits as well as your capabilities.

Let your stimulants come from within you.

Seek not to know who said
this or that, but take note of
what has been said.

Thomas à Kempis

**Try always to bring out
the best in yourself and
in others.**

Make time for yourself.

Give loving
encouragement
to yourself.

**Learn that you are the best friend
you will ever have.**

Strive to be at peace with yourself.

Our life is the result of our thoughts. If we can understand this, then we can change our life for the better anytime we choose.

When we can control our thoughts, we can control the manifestations of our thoughts.

Always remind yourself of the importance of slowing down. Not only you, but everything you do, will benefit from it.

**Once you have found peace
and harmony in your life
it will stay with you always,
like your shadow.**

Our life is vital and part of
something infinite, so how can
we contemplate our mortality
when what we are is infinite?

A lust for possessions is no different from any other form of lust.

If we can control our desires, we can find peace.

We can work for the sake of work, or we can work at some productive endeavor. One way will lead to a peaceful life, the other will lead away from it.

Remain steadfast.
A tree with shallow roots will fall given the gentlest breeze— no amount of wind can topple a mountain.

Try to learn to differentiate
between what you want and
what you need.

**What's been said is enough
for anyone with sense.**

Who can find peace and harmony in their life and yet remain untruthful?

Who that has no self-restraint can find peace and harmony in their life?

Tell a lie
and live
a lie.

**Think a
lie and
live a lie.**

Don't accept that stress is an inevitable part of modern life.

Peace and harmony elude the confused.

We can never achieve a peaceful life if we seek it in things.

Strive to remain, moment
to moment, centered in
the oneness of infinity.

If we are not careful,
our preoccupation
with stress and
anxiety will deprive
us of enjoying the
fullness of life.

Meditate on our oneness
with the earth.

**Meditate on our oneness
with the universe.**

Meditate on our oneness
with all of humanity.

The greatest treasure any living person can have is their vigilance.

Avoid becoming sidetracked by too many sensuous pleasures.

You are as important as any other thing in creation.

Consider a peaceful life as a still, safe harbor where no storm, no matter how violent, can touch us.

There is no old and no young
in meditation.

When we meditate
we are all things,
we are infinite.

Negligence is always avoided by the wise.

He that is born to be hanged shall never need fear drowning.

Don't step in a puddle
while you are busy
gazing at the stars.

**Meditation helps us
to separate our mind
from confusion.**

Confusion is poison
to a peaceful life.

If left
undisciplined,
the mind will
wander.

Avoid allowing the mind to become confused.

When we feel fear it is good to meditate on our oneness with good and evil.

No matter how frail or fragile our body, we can still fortify our mind.

Overindulge in any pleasure, and it will carry off the mind in confusion of thought as surely as the wind will steal a kite from its careless handler.

One step backward is further than a dozen steps forward.

A single night can seem an eternity to one who cannot sleep.

A mile might as well be twenty miles to one who is weary with travel.

The road is always steepest just before you glimpse the lights of home.

Those who are confused are enemies to themselves. Their thoughts and their actions only serve to increase their confusion.

Deeds done in confusion cause regret.

Act in good faith.

When we are confused, everything sounds like the truth.

Ask yourself if you really
want to reach the top.
From there you will have a
long way to travel to
socialize with the peaceful
people in the valley below.

Do not waste your life wishing for reputation.

Do not waste your life wishing for high rank in society.

One person's stepping stone is another person's destination.

Do not judge others by your own standards.

True friends will help us to remain on our life path.

False friends will cause us to stray from our life path.

**We are the authors
of our thoughts.**

Nothing of lasting value may be
attained by wrongful means.

Abandon the
darkness of
confusion
and live in
the light of
peace and
harmony.

Enjoy solitude—there is peace and harmony to be found there.

A single peaceful word is better than a thousand speeches.

A peaceful verse is worth a thousand empty poems.

If we have not quiet in our minds, outward comfort will do no more for us than a golden slipper on a gouty foot.

If each was to conquer self then none would wish to conquer any other.

One hour spent meditating on nature is worth more than an entire lifetime with our senses closed.

Do not squander life.

You do not need a whip to urge on an obedient horse.

Everything comes to fruition.
Who can hold back the
flowers at springtime?
Let him hold back the ocean.

**Difficulties along the path
of life are opportunities.**

Though each path is
different, there is only
one way.

**Even the loftiest of
mountains begins with
its feet on the ground.**

If you are patient in one moment of anger, you will escape a hundred days of sorrow.

Think twice and act once.

After three days
without reading,
talk loses its flavor.

Keep an open mind.

Never correct with a strike that which can be taught with a kiss.

We need not fear desire, only try to understand it.

The greatest gift we can give to ourselves and to others is truth.

Instead of cursing the darkness,
light a candle.

Are those who do not read
any better off than those
who cannot read?

Craving is like a river
in flood.

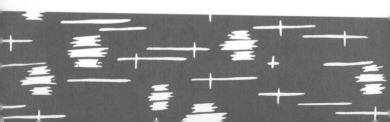

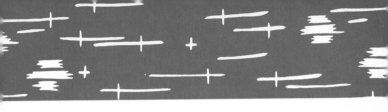

From quiet reflection effective action flows.

With an eye made quiet by the power of harmony, and the deep power of joy, we see into the life of things.

William Wordsworth

All that is noble is in itself of a quiet nature, and appears to sleep until it is aroused and summoned forth by contrast.

Johann Wolfgang von Goethe

Go with
the Flow

No person can absolutely make an opportunity.

Courage itself is not enough.

An infinity of excuses can always be found for nonaction.

We strive to achieve, seeking out the places where we can distinguish ourselves.
Imagine if life itself was that very place and that everything was possible.

When opportunity comes, be prepared so that you can see it instantly and use it correctly.

By working faithfully eight hours a day, you may eventually get to be boss and work twelve.

Robert Frost

Anticipation is a form of positive stress.

Positive stress can add excitement to life. We all thrive under a certain amount of stress.

Without some positive stress our lives can become dull or boring, and we may even become depressed.

Think of competition, deadlines, frustration, and even confrontation as the spice of life.

Sorrow adds depth to life and fear enriches it.

Our goal should not be to eliminate stress from our lives, rather to learn how to manage it.

Ask this: how can I use this moment of stress to my advantage?

Too much of any kind of stress can place us in a state of turmoil or tie us up in knots.

Too much pressure and we become easily overwhelmed, but the right amount can actually be motivating.

We all react to stress differently, so we must each learn what our optimal stress level is and how to recognize it.

We are all individual creatures and have unique needs.

One person's Ode to Joy is another's cause of distress.

The amount of stress we can tolerate alters as we grow older; so too does the amount of stress we require.

It is said that unrelieved stress is the underlying factor of most illness.

Stress can help compel us to action, but we must make sure it is the right action.

Stress can allow us a new perspective on things.

There are many sources of stress, and as many ways to manage it.

Identify the sources of your stress,
be aware of its effect upon you,
and then learn to manage it.

What causes me anxiety, and what are my reactions to it?

Glossing over our problems will not
ease the distress they cause us.

Notice distress.
Never ignore it.

We can all learn to recognize
what things we can and must
change in ourselves.

A key factor in the management of stress is our ability, and desire, to reduce our emotional reactions to stress.

To learn something and then to utilize it gives one a harmonious sense of attainment.

To have friends come from far away to visit is uplifting.

To be indifferent to recognition by others of one's talents is the keystone to a life of peace and harmony.

If a person concentrates on achieving harmony as the root of their life and that root is firmly planted, then the harmony surrounding them will increase.

In my acts for others, have I been worthy of their trust?

When you make a mistake, admit it immediately and endeavor to correct it.

Be in harmony with your promises and you will be able to fulfill them.

In your interactions with people, be in harmony with their customs and traditions.

Everything should be made as simple as possible, but not simpler.
Albert Einstein

Every human being, to some extent, lives in confusion.

A rash is a rash
whatever
expensive material
you cloak over it.

**There can be
no reasoning
with despair.**

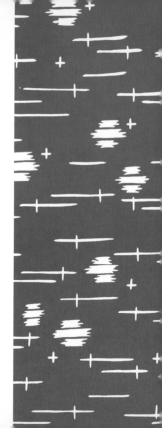

We travel through life clothing everything we come across in human meaning. If we recognize that, then we can soon see that at the heart everything is truly inhuman.

Nothing can drive mankind to the extremes of emotion more quickly than beauty.

We have to somehow overcome our self-centred desires if we are going to achieve a peaceful life.

Why live as if our only task on earth was to make our own way easier?

Sometimes it takes us a tremendous amount of energy just to be normal.

You will never be happy if you continue to search for what happiness consists of. You will never live if you are looking for the meaning of life.

Albert Camus

What is a happy peaceful life except the simple harmony between man and the life he leads?

The greatest sin against life is wishing for another life.

Sometimes we must be prepared to give away a little of our life in order not to lose it all.

Every reason we can give for dying is also the reason for living.

Not understanding is altogether different from refusing to know.

Beauty, love, and danger are each so overwhelming that it is hardly any wonder that a peaceful life is so hard to come by.

Farming looks easy when your plow is a pencil and you're a thousand miles from a cornfield.

Dwight D. Eisenhower

Many feel they go through life not knowing themselves. It takes a lifetime to fashion a personality, but the moment we know ourselves perfectly we die.

We are not certain, we are never certain.

Why should anyone take us seriously?

Of all the creatures of this earth mankind is the only one who point blankly refuses to be what he is.

Iron rusts from disuse, stagnant water loses its purity, and in cold weather becomes frozen, even so does inaction sap the vigors of the mind.

Leonardo da Vinci

Nothing is quite
so vulgar as a
person's need
to be right.

We can live a
peaceful life when we
can indulge in
pleasures without
becoming a slave to
any of them.

Justice denies freedom.

**We are always fidgeting and
never quite satisfied.**

Give someone a fish and
they'll ask for a lemon.

**Teach someone to fish and they'll
never starve.
Teach someone to fish and they'll
leave work early on Friday!**

If you want to move a mountain you must begin by carting away small stones.

There are those who like to work and there are those who like to take the credit.

Forget and forgive. This is not difficult when properly understood. It means forget inconvenient duties, then forgive yourself for forgetting. By rigid practice and stern determination, it comes easy.

Mark Twain

Wasting time is an important part of living.

The burden is equal to the horse's strength.
the Talmud

Some of us go on at length about things we feel we have no time to be brief about.

When spider webs unite, they can tie up a lion.
Ethiopian proverb

Sometimes a lifetime of doubt can be eased by a couple of peaceful hours in the library.

The sooner you fall behind, the more time you have to catch up.

For most of us, if we didn't leave things until the very last moment then nothing would get done at all.

For a man to achieve all that is demanded of him, he must regard himself as greater than he is.

Johann Wolfgang von Goethe

Either allow time
to do it right or
time to do it over.

If you truly love your job, you will never have to work another day in your life.

It is more honorable to fail at something than to excel in doing nothing.

The quickest way usually
takes a long time to discover.

**Don't minimize your contribution.
All jobs appear easy to the person
who doesn't have to do them.**

Whatever you do will be insignificant,
but it is very important that you do it.

Mahatma Gandhi

The key to doing what you like in this life is to like whatever it is you do.

Those who are genuinely busy will never have time to tell you how busy they are.

The important thing is not to confuse your quest for a peaceful life with laziness.

A peaceful life will allow us to achieve more and greater things.

Laziness achieves nothing.

Don't wait for death to tell you to slow down.

Music exists as noise in disarray until a musician shapes it.

Next time you see your colleagues in a flurry of furious activity, before being impressed ask yourself if they understand what it is they are doing.

Do not permit the events of your daily life to bind you, but never withdraw yourself from them.

Zen saying

**The same river runs both ways;
we can go with the flow or swim
against the stream.**

The artist is nothing without the gift,
but the gift is nothing without work.

Emile Zola

Rarely is anything
impromptu unprepared.

Alone we can start in our own time.
Together we must wait for each other.

**Forgive and forget,
and save yourself all
that wasted energy.**

Many who thought they were on the right
track have been hit by a train that wasn't.

One of the symptoms of an approaching nervous breakdown is the belief that one's work is terribly important.

Bertrand Russell

All too often when we reach the point in life that we wished to reach we find ourselves wishing we were that person we were at that point in our lives when we wished to be what we have now become.

We must ask ourselves, what is the something else we would rather be doing?

Wherever you are, and whatever you are doing, use what you have, to do what you can.

The beginning is the most important part.

Plato

When we value ourselves we find that we begin to value our time. Before this, time is meaningless and we are wasteful with it.

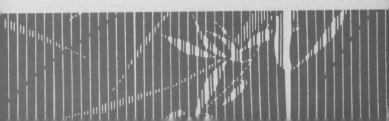

To create the illusion of progress organizations like to meet each new situation by reorganizing.

Sometimes we travel furthest while standing still.

You will break the bow if you keep it always stretched.

Phaedrus

People tend to remember a job well done, not a bad job done swiftly.

If you allow it to, your workload will expand to fill every moment of available time.

A journey of a thousand miles must begin with a single step.

Lao-Tzu

Cherish comfort and you will never have a peaceful life.

Success can be measured by the number of telephones in your home, peace can be measured by how few.

Forget how others judge us, for their judgment is based only upon what we have done.

We must be our own judge, and our judgment should be based upon what we feel we are capable of doing.

Success is not all it's cracked up to be.

It is neither wealth nor splendor,
but tranquillity and occupation,
that gives happiness.

Thomas Jefferson

Some view success as receiving payment for doing something they might despise.

For others it is just enough to do what they love doing.

We are often trapped into thinking that the wonderful feeling of accomplishment can only be attained by completing some task or duty. It can also be attained by letting go of everything external and allowing yourself to unite with the moment.

The only way to get around a problem is to work your way through it.

From the cradle to the grave we trundle through life weighed down by feelings of necessity.

Bear in mind that the person who does something great owes a great debt to the faithful work of others.

We must sail sometimes with the wind and sometimes against it—but we must sail, and not drift, nor lie at anchor.
Oliver Wendell Holmes

Opportunity is missed by most people because it is dressed in overalls and looks like work.

Thomas Alva Edison

Learn to be poor without succumbing to an attitude of subservience and rich without being arrogant.

All are equal if consciousness is common.

It is important to enjoy one's own company.

If the life we want to be a part of doesn't exist, sometimes we have to create it.

There is no beginning to practice nor end to enlightenment; There is no beginning to enlightenment nor end to practice.

Dogen

What is the meaning
of life?
   the moon
   the trees
   a long night.

Standing
Still

Still your mind, still yourself, and unite with the love that dwells in your heart.

Meditation is universal and sublime. It does not belong to any particular sect or cult, any age, race, or country. It exists for the benefit of all people.

Learn to know what leads you forward and also that which holds you back.

In your moments of choice, try always to choose the path that leads to wisdom.

Through meditation and developing the ability to give full attention to one thing at a time, we can train ourselves to direct our attention wherever we choose.

In deep meditation the flow of concentration is continuous like the flow of oil.

Patanjali

We have within each of us the power to make ourselves whatever we wish to be.

Take care about what you think—we are what our thoughts make us.

Thoughts live and they can travel far.

The most powerful person is he who has himself in his own power.

All fears and all boundless miseries originate from the mind.

Those who know others are intelligent; those who know themselves are truly wise. Those who master others are strong; those who master themselves have true power.

Lao-Tzu

It is not possible for us to restrain the external course of things; but if we can restrain our mind there becomes no need to restrain anything else.

Those of us who wish to find a peaceful life and overcome misery must comprehend the secret of the mind.

We must look within
ourselves if we are
to overcome the
present.

Meditation can help us to
liberate ourselves to reach a
level of internal stability, a state
of spiritual balance.

Inside each of us lies the path to mental peace.

Imagine feeling yourself to be free of grief, free of fear, and alive without anxiety.

Elusive and unreliable as it is, the wise man straightens out his restless, agitated mind, like a fletcher crafting an arrow.

Buddha

We all have it within ourselves to rise from feelings of complete hopelessness to a state of renewed strength, clarity, understanding, and peace.

Seek, and
ye shall find;
knock, and
it shall be
opened unto
you.

Matthew 7:7

Meditate and you will feel wonderful and enriched.

Through meditation we can feel ourselves become new in a moment.

Meditate and disturbing influences upon the mind soon vanish.

Meditate and discover within you a peaceful fountain of bliss.

Meditation is like peacefully swimming in an ocean of knowledge and understanding everything.

Meditation is suitable for people of all temperaments and for all times.

Meditation brings peace and solace to souls that are afflicted by the three fires of mortal existence: afflictions caused by one's own body; those caused by beings around one; and those caused by the unseen.

Meditation brings wisdom, lack of meditation leaves ignorance.

Meditation can be a constant companion of life.

You will find that you will acquire in meditation deeper knowledge, insight, and clearer thinking, as well as reducing feelings of doubt.

The enemies of a peaceful life are the mind, ego, impressions, senses, cravings, likes, dislikes, lust, jealousy, greed, pride, and hypocrisy.

My Self is hidden here in
this body just as there is fire
hidden in wood or cheese
hidden in milk.

Try to control your
likes and dislikes.

The Self is the witness of the mind.

The Self is the ruler of life breath. From the Self nothing can be hidden.

It is a waste of time arguing about the "why" and "wherefore" of life.

Use the present in such a way that time itself could be conquered.

That is wisdom.

Have no fear of the Self.

Elevate, enlighten, guide, and protect me.

Remove the obstacles on my spiritual path.

Remove the veil of ignorance.

Prayer to Lord Krishna

The happy person in this world is not bound by conventions.

The quest for rational knowledge paves the path to peaceful life.

Where there is charity and wisdom, there is neither fear nor ignorance.

Where there is patience and humility, there is neither anger nor vexation.

Where there is poverty and joy, there is neither greed nor avarice.

Where there is peace and meditation, there is neither anxiety nor doubt.

St. Francis of Assisi

Give up trying to know what is on God's mind.

Never cease to be amazed at the harmony of natural law.

We should widen our circle of compassion to embrace all living creatures and the whole of nature in all its beauty.

Intuition and rationality are the yin and yang of the mind.

Nature reveals a superior intelligence which makes the systematic thinking and actions of humans seem totally insignificant.

Intellect should never be worshiped as our God.

Peace cannot be kept by force. It can only be achieved by understanding.

Never stop questioning. Our curiosity exists for a reason.

Meditate upon nature and experience the feeling of humility.

We can only ever hope to come to understand a minute fraction of the mysteries that surround us. Be satisfied with this.

The real problem is in the hearts and minds of men. It is easier to denature plutonium than to denature the evil spirit of man.

Albert Einstein

Virtue is strength, power, and the key to peace.

A virtuous man is happy, peaceful, and prosperous.

Be tranquil within.

All that we can hope for is that
we will do the right thing at the
right moment.

Treat even the
lowliest creatures
with respect.

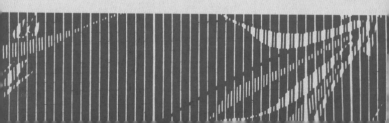

Let your words agree with
your thoughts.

**Let your actions agree with
your words.**

Be simple in your speech. Do not twist your words and topics. Be plain; avoid being cunning or crooked.

Be simple in your food. Be simple in your dress. Try it.

Speak softly and be precise in what you say.

Be truthful. Think twice before you speak. Stick to promises. Never exaggerate or twist facts.

Be calm when faced with injury, suffering, failure, or disrespect.

Be calm when faced with praise, pleasure, or success.

Let nothing disturb your inner peace.

Consider no being as inferior to you.

Once you set out on the path to a peaceful life, stick to it. Remain steadfast. Never waver.

Try to seek out the good qualities in everyone.

Cultivate a healthy interest in art, and art will cultivate in you a good conscience and a powerful imagination.

Never look for fault in others.

Try not to let the mind dwell on insignificant things.

Try to radiate thoughts of goodness and love.

Forgive.
Life
is too
short to
bear a
grudge.

Nothing is so praiseworthy, nothing so clearly shows a great and noble soul, as clemency and readiness to forgive.

Cicero

The mistakes of the past are our torches for the present.

Great people talk about ideas.
Small people talk about other
people.

**Don't give up. It is always
within our power to change
our nature.**

**Always remember even Mozart,
Isaac Newton, Charles Darwin,
Leonardo da Vinci, and Albert
Einstein made mistakes.**

When no one really cares about who will get the credit, then a team can really accomplish something.

You cannot motivate a person to become as they could be by treating them only as they are.

Walk humbly through life.

Don't worry. The deepest-rooted principle common to all human nature is the longing to be appreciated.

Memory is the child of interest. Arouse the attention, feed the interest, and memory will play its role.

The desire to acquire great wealth is in itself a kind of insanity.

Why waste our energy, our thoughts, and our lives striving to acquire what we don't need?

Obstacles and problems are part of life. A peaceful life is merely about changing our relationship to them.

Most misery is produced by ignorance.

Consider the various religions of the world as different viewpoints of the same Truth.

Detach the mind from the objects.

Not only in nature does one feel the spirit rejuvenated by what one sees, but also in the magnificent creations of mankind.

Be good, do good. Four little words that sum up ethics.

I have not sought during my life to amass wealth and to adorn my body, but I have sought to adorn my soul with the jewels of wisdom, patience, and above all with a love of liberty.

Socrates

The peaceful life we seek does not consist of running away from duties and responsibilities. It is purely an internal state that any person may visit while living amidst the confusion of the world.

A weak spot anywhere in the structure can ruin the whole.

True peace is truly a state of mind.

That which you cannot change, accept.

Free your heart, be generous
and never miserly.

**Find joy in the happiness that you
can bring to others.**

Try to remain pure
at heart.

Try to eradicate lust, anger,
and greed from your thoughts.

Let me
love,
give,
serve,
purify,
meditate,
realize.

When embarking on a course of action, consider the well-being of all.

Do nothing and evil will triumph.

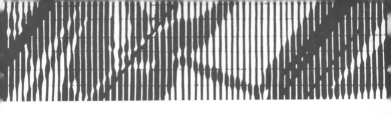

Accept evil and you are guilty of cooperating with evil.

Remember that although you cannot do everything, you can do something.

If we think happy thoughts,
we will be happy.

If we think miserable thoughts,
we will be miserable.

Dale Carnegie

**Give up trying to be absolutely
right, and seek only to be less
wrong than the generations that
have gone before.**

In an ever-changing world change is what is needed.

The fainthearted fear change.

How can we be really living if we don't grow? If we are to grow, we have to be prepared to change.

Madness is
the result not of
uncertainty but
certainty.
Friedrich Nietzsche

**Most of the worst
crimes in history
have been
committed against
humanity in the
name of certainty.**

An argument can never be won with insults.

It takes strength and courage to show kindness.

Any fool can criticize, condemn, and complain— and most fools do.

Dale Carnegie

Ask yourself if you have the character and self-control to be understanding and forgiving.

Where there is kindness you will also discover greatness.

Kindness reforms and ennobles.

It takes will to keep emotion under the control of reason.

No man can afford to keep a viper of revenge in his heart.

Remember that enthusiasm was behind everything great that was ever achieved.

We can feel instantly peaceful within the moment we choose not to feel compelled to prove ourselves to others.

The world is not unreal; but it is a lesser reality than the Self.

Stop for a moment.

Close your eyes.

It is late autumn.

See a tree.

It has only one leaf gently moving in the breeze,

 beside it a single apple.

Stop for a moment.

Close your eyes.

It is late autumn.

See a tree.

It has only one leaf gently moving in the breeze,

   beside it a single apple.

See the apple fall from the branch to the ground.

Stop for a moment.

Close your eyes.

It is late autumn.

See a tree.

It has only one leaf gently moving in the breeze,

   beside it a single apple.

See the apple fall from the branch and hold it in mid-air.

Balance your mind
in pain and joy.

Free the
Spirit

Avoid negativity and being negative towards others.

When a person grows up surrounded by tolerance, they learn to be patient.

Try to temper your excess emotions.

It is one thing to show a man that he is in an error, and another to put him in the position of the truth.

John Locke

Train the mind to meditate.

When a person grows up surrounded by acceptance and friendship, they learn to find love in the world.

God must love the common man because he makes so many of them.

I am the proud owner of this body.

The proud are easily offended.

Make a life of peace and harmony your goal. It is more difficult than it sounds.

To err is human, to forgive divine.

Alexander Pope

Anger is an expensive luxury.

No power so effectively robs the mind of all its powers of acting and reasoning as fear.

Edmund Burke

Deal with the faults of others as gently as with your own.

Since we cannot get what we like, let us like what we can get.

Good advice is often annoying, bad advice never.

He who knows nothing, doubts nothing.

The life is short, the craft so long to learn.

Hippocrates

It is easy to be wise after the event.

A spoon does not know the taste of soup, nor does a learned fool know the taste of wisdom.

A lie travels round the world in the time it takes truth to put its boots on.

Give a man a chance to steal before you judge him honest.

True knowledge lies in knowing how to live.

Baltasar Gracián

The human language is like a cracked kettle on which we beat out a tune for a dancing bear, when we hope with our music to move the stars.

Gustave Flaubert

If a person is peaceful, even their dog will be peaceful.

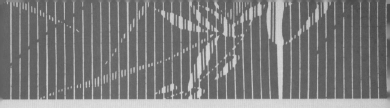

Imagination is more important than knowledge.

When the facts are in hiding, the experts appear.

Bad habits are like a comfortable bed; easy to get into, but hard to get out of.

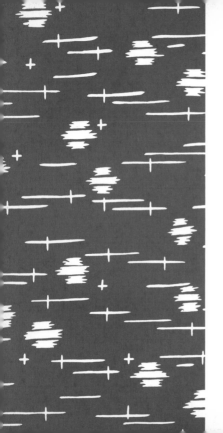

When you meet a man, judge him by his clothes; when you leave a man, judge him by his heart.

They are not dead who live in the hearts they leave behind.

He knows the world and does not know himself.

Jean de La Fontaine

The end is the crown of any work.

The mind has a thousand eyes,
And the heart but one;
Yet the light of a whole life dies
When love is done.

Francis Bourdillon

I do not know what I may appear to the world; but to myself I seem to have been only like a boy playing on the sea-shore, and diverting myself in now and then finding a smoother pebble or a prettier shell than ordinary, whilst the great ocean of truth lay all undiscovered before me.

Isaac Newton

Lord, what fools these mortals be!

William Shakespeare

Find something
uplifting in all that
you do.

One hand washes the other.

The eyes are the
mirror of the soul.

Every man is dragged on by his favorite pleasure.

Virgil

To ask is no sin and to be refused is no calamity.

Ask yourself whether you are happy and you cease to be so.

Hugo Meynell

No one is dragged to heaven by the hair.

Have faith in yourself.

No man's pleasure should have to depend upon the permission of another.

If solid happiness we prize,
Within our breast this jewel lies,
And they are fools who roam.
The world has nothing to bestow;
From our own selves our joys must flow,
And that dear hut, our home.

Nathaniel Cotton

**Happiness is not a horse.
You cannot harness it.**

Find the ability to pardon.

Humility is a virtue all preach,
none practice; and yet
everybody is content to hear.
John Selden

A half-truth is a whole lie.

Some rise by sin, and some by virtue fall.

William Shakespeare

Surrounding yourself with dwarfs will never make you a giant and vice versa.

Bygone troubles are good to tell.

You can't step twice into the same river.

Heraclitus

If the rich could hire someone else to die for them, the poor would make a wonderful living.

The first of earthly blessings, independence.

Virgil

A little rule, a little sway,
A sunbeam in a winter's day,
Is all the proud and mighty have
Between the cradle and the
grave.

John Dyer

If we each were to take a step towards a more peaceful life, we would come closer to a time when man's inhumanity towards fellow man would cease.

**Death hath a thousand doors
to let out life.**

Philip Massinger

All this is so obvious that it
ought not to be necessary
to repeat it.

When your roof burns down, enjoy the chance to see the moon from your bed.

I, a stranger and afraid, in
a world I never made.
                    A.E. Housman

Ask the bird perched sleeping in the church bell tower about peaceful moments.

The noblest mind the best
contentment has.
                    Edmund Spenser

Try not to swat bees while praying.

Sitting peacefully doing nothing, Spring comes and the grass grows all by itself.

You do not need to leave your room. Remain sitting at your table and listen. Do not even listen, simply wait. Do not even wait, be still and solitary. The world will freely offer itself to you to be unmasked, it has no choice. It will roll in ecstasy at your feet.

Franz Kafka

The ability to see things normally is no small thing.

If no one binds you then why seek liberation?

Meditation is both the means and the end.

Poverty is no disgrace to a man, but it is confoundedly inconvenient.

Sydney Smith

That which remains when there is no more grasping is the Self.

To learn we must step from
the known into the unknown.

**It is not the pot but the emptiness
inside it that holds the contents.**

Zen is merely the art of
the uncovering of inherent
knowledge.

Do your work, then step back.
The only path to serenity.

Lao-Tzu

**Would that we had spent one day
well in this world!**

Thomas à Kempis

Being is what it is.

Jean-Paul Sartre

The worst wound we can be asked to endure is that of self-criticism.

Better it is to live one day strenuous and resolute than to live a hundred years sluggish and dissipated.

The noblest victor is he who conquers himself.

Zen is seeing into one's own nature.

Hui-neng

Simplicity is a terribly complicated thing to try and understand.

An inch of time is an inch of gold: treasure it. Appreciate its fleeting nature; misplaced gold is easily found, misspent time is lost forever.

Loy Ching-Yuen

No god or devil can upset the peace achieved by those who have succeeded in subduing themselves.

Better it is to live one day virtuous and meditative than to live a hundred years immoral and uncontrolled.

Where there is despair let there be hope.

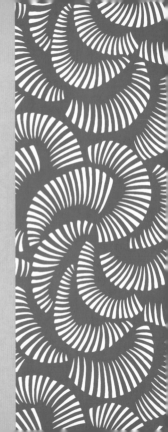

Let the joy and light of self-knowledge into your life and drive out the dark sadness of uncertainty.

When I hear I see, when I see I hear.
Zen koan

Seek to understand and to be understood.

We are here and it is now. Further than that all human knowledge is moonshine.

H. L. Mencken

One can attain peace in a single useful word.

Sow an act, and you reap a habit. Sow a habit, and you reap a character, sow a character, and you reap a destiny.

Charles Reade

The danger is believing that our self-image is who we actually are.

Our greatest fear is the fear of emotion.

Let go of false beliefs and feel the weight fall from your shoulders.

If you try to aim for it, you are turning away from it.

Zen master

If you wish to drown, do not torture yourself with shallow water.

If you do not get it from yourself, where will you go for it?

Zen saying

Be an instrument of peace.

Learn to love most where you hate most.

The love of liberty is the love of others; the love of power is the love of ourselves.

William Hazlitt

It is vital to recognize what you are not, in order that what you really are can naturally emerge.

Whatever you can do, or dream you can, begin it. Boldness has genius, power, and magic in it. Begin it now.

Johann Wolfgang von Goethe

No one is old until they think old.

Old age is the most unexpected of all the things that can happen to a man.

Leon Trotsky

We're lost if we are only as real as the character we establish.

Your peaceful life is right where you are now. If you seek it elsewhere, you will not find it.

You see, but you do not observe.

Sir Arthur Conan Doyle

How long will the ripples of
our life remain after we have
left this life?

**It is said that the meek shall inherit
the earth. It's then up to them to
keep hold of it.**

**All that is human must retrograde
if it does not advance.**

Edward Gibbon

Credulous hope supports our life,
and always says that tomorrow will
be better.

Tibullus

The most positive men are the most credulous.

Alexander Pope

Do anything when you are in a temper, and you will do everything wrong.

Let the first impulse pass, wait for the second.

Baltasar Gracián

Self-criticism is self-hatred. Without exception it will hurt you.

No one else can change you, only you can change yourself.

Everyone who is successful must have dreamed of something.

The joys we expect are not so bright, nor the troubles so dark as we fancy they will be.

Charles Reade

Sometimes being alone is the best company you can have.

Not how long, but how well you have lived is the main thing.

Seneca

The secret of joy is contained in one word—excellence. Know how to do something well and enjoy it.

Be peaceful in your aspirations.

Sorrow and silence are strong,
patient endurance is godlike.

Henry Wadsworth Longfellow

To be at ease is better than to be at
business. Nothing really belongs to
us but time, which even he has who
has nothing else.

Baltasar Gracián

Time Out

Our stillness must be found from within. Always remember that we are standing on a ball that is hurtling through space.

Consider your life as an ocean and remember that water that is too pure will not sustain fish.

Great doubt,
great awakening.

**Small doubt,
small awakening.**

No doubt,
no awakening.

Try not to torment yourself afresh
with the memory of what is past.

**Do not afflict yourself with the
apprehension of evils to come.**

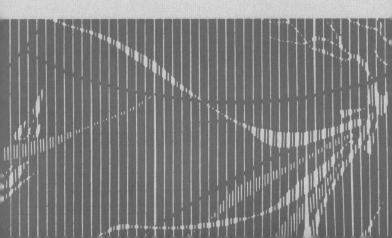

**One should count each day
a separate life.**

Seneca

Beware of taking as real all
that is nonexistent.

It is better to
practice a little
than to talk a lot.

**Everything
the same;
everything
distinct.**
Zen saying

Don't give up. In a hundred-mile march, ninety is about halfway.

Many people will walk in and out of your life, but only true friends will leave footprints on your heart.

To handle yourself,
use your head.
To handle others,
use your heart.

**Anger and danger are two
parts of the same word.**

If someone betrays you once, it is his fault. If he betrays you twice, it is your fault.

Before you speak, make sure your brain is in gear.

He who loses money,
loses much.
He who loses a friend,
loses much more.

He who loses faith,
loses all.

**Beautiful young people are
accidents of nature, but beautiful
old people are works of art.**

Learn from the mistakes of others; you can't live long enough to make them all yourself.

Yesterday is history.
Tomorrow is a mystery.
Today is a gift.

Suffering is the surest sign that you are alive.

Nothing can bring you peace
but yourself.

Ralph Waldo Emerson

**I'm an idealist. I don't know where
I'm going, but I'm on my way.**

Carl Sandburg

A man cannot be comfortable
without his own approval.

Mark Twain

Everyone smiles in the same language.

If you wish to be like someone else, you waste the person you are.

Nostalgia is the realization that things weren't as unbearable as they seemed at the time.

To live a perfect life,
you must ask nothing,
give nothing, and
expect nothing.

Waste not fresh tears
over old griefs.

Violence is the last refuge
of the incompetent.

Isaac Asimov

**You should never wear your best
trousers when you go out to fight
for freedom and liberty.**

Henrik Ibsen

Remember that to our foes, it
is we who are the enemy.

Sometimes the only winning move is not to play.

In war there are no winners, only losers.

The only thing we have to fear is fear itself.
Franklin D. Roosevelt

It is impossible to defend absolutely against the attack of those who wish to die.

Mankind seems intent upon exhausting all other possibilities before accepting the course of acting rationally.

When elephants fight, only the grass gets hurt.

There is nothing so easy but that it becomes difficult when you do it reluctantly.

Terence

We like to trust those who agree with us, but remember an enemy will happily agree with everything we say, while a true friend is more likely to argue.

All paid jobs absorb and
degrade the mind.

Aristotle

Try to relax and
enjoy the crisis.

I love deadlines. I like the whooshing sound they make as they fly by.

Douglas Adams

Some will never put off until tomorrow what can be done today, others will never put off until tomorrow what they can avoid altogether.

The best leaders will say what it is that has to be done and then leave you to apply your own methods to provide the results.

Happiness in comfort is not real happiness. When you can be happy in the midst of hardship, then you see the true potential of the mind.

Wonder is the beginning of wisdom.

To ask the
hard question
is simple.
      W. H. Auden

Calm in quietude is not real calm; when you can be calm in the midst of activity, that is the true state of nature.

On the edge of the forest
Live joyfully,
Without desire.

Buddha

Which would be worse,
a day without food or
a day without work?

A day without work is a day without eating.

Pai-chang

Can you imagine any greater curse than having every wish you made come true?

In one ear and out many mouths. So a rumor goes.

Nothing dries sooner than tears.

Which is better, a teacher or two books?

Where people fail in their search for a peaceful life is that they set out to find it as though it were some form of excitement when they should merely concentrate upon everyday routine and the moment.

Why should a drowning man worry about rain?

It is better to conceal one's knowledge than to reveal one's ignorance.

We must learn to look at peace as being more than a period of turmoil that sits between wars.

The man who strikes first admits that his ideas have given out.

Learn to stand back from your life and take stock.

When you feel you are approaching the end of your journey, that is really only the beginning.

Experience gives the test first and the lesson afterwards.

The shell must break before the bird can fly.
Alfred, Lord Tennyson

Your vision will become clear only when you can look into your own heart. Who looks outside, dreams; who looks inside, awakes.

Carl Jung

A smart person knows what to say, a wise person knows whether or not to say it.

What greater joy can there be than the realization that your life is being used for a great purpose?

Accept now that the world will not go out of its way to make you happy.

If you bring forth what is within you, it will heal you. And if you do not bring forth what is within you, it will destroy you.

Gospel of St. Thomas

Be loyal to your values.

Learn to know when it is important to please yourself first.

Rid yourself of anger and resentment.

Go to your bosom: knock there, and ask your heart what it doth know.

William Shakespeare

Learn to accept that pain is part of life.

No pressure—no diamonds!

We fear that what is going on now is going to go on forever. It's not so—no problem lasts forever.

The intellect has little to do on the road to discovery. There comes a leap in consciousness, call it intuition or what you will, and the solution comes to you and you don't know how or why.

Albert Einstein

To some, the harder they work the more they live, and the easier it is for them to find a peaceful life.

Rejoice in life for its own sake.

We do not see things as they are; we see things as we are.

the Talmud

Life is either a daring adventure or nothing.

Helen Keller

Those who are happiest go to their death thoroughly used up.

Hope is not the conviction that something will turn out well but the certainty that something makes sense, regardless of how it turns out.

Vaclav Havel

Try to live fully and simply in the present moment.

Life is no "brief candle" to me. It is a sort of splendid torch which I have got hold of for the moment, and I want to make it burn as brightly as possible before handing it on to future generations.

George Bernard Shaw

Try to understand that contentment is not about fulfiling your wants but a realization of what you already have.

If you understand, things are just as they are; if you do not understand, things are just as they are.

Zen proverb

There are a thousand reasons to worry and twice as many not to.

We should not hurry, we should not be impatient, but we should confidently obey the eternal rhythm.

Nikos Kazantzakis

Anxiety breeds anxiety. Step out of the vicious circle.

Free yourself to express your ideas and feelings. Don't bottle them up inside you.

There are two ways to live your life. One is as though nothing is a miracle. The other is as though everything is a miracle.

Albert Einstein

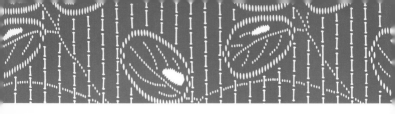

Try to keep in touch with old friends.

Always remain realistic in your expectations.

Try to make healthy choices.

Be grateful for
your blessings.

**Recognize your
responsibilities to others.**

Just as you have the right to live your own life, others have a right to live their own lives.

Listen—not just with your ears, but with your heart.

Share joy as well as sorrow.

Above all,
don't
cause
pain.

As the ripples on a pond follow the splash of a thrown pebble, everything we do creates echoes. Take care, for everything matters.

In this life pain is inevitable but suffering is optional.

Don't fall into the trap of basing all your thoughts and actions on fears of past experiences. Free yourself, learn to think and act with spontaneity.

Those who have found the way have an unmistakable ability to enjoy each moment.

**We will be nearer to living
a peaceful life when we lose
all interest in judging others.**

We will be nearer to
living a peaceful life
when we lose
interest in analyzing
the actions of others.

We will be nearer to living a peaceful life when we lose interest in conflict.

We will be nearer to living a peaceful life when we lose our conditioned need to worry.

We will be nearer to living a peaceful life when we experience frequent episodes of appreciation.

We will be nearer to living a peaceful life when we experience feelings of contentment.

We will be nearer to living a peaceful life when we feel our connection with other people and with nature.

We will be nearer to living a peaceful life when we discover our desire to smile more often.

We will be nearer to living a peaceful life when we feel less need to make things happen.

We will be nearer to living a peaceful life when we recognize the love extended by others and our reciprocal feelings.

We are born into this life with a body which we choose to love or hate.

Consider life as a university full of opportunities for discovery and learning.

Consider that in life there are no mistakes, only lessons to be learned.

No part of life does not
contain its lessons.

We come into this life equipped
with all the necessary resources to
make a life. It is up to each of us to
make what we want of our lives.

When a person grows up surrounded by criticism, they learn to condemn.

When a person grows up surrounded by hostility, they learn to fight.

It is perfectly right to accept love from others, even when we don't love ourselves very much.

The answer to life's questions are within us if we look and listen with our heart and trust in our own judgment.

Published by MQ Publications Limited
12 The Ivories, 6–8 Northampton Street
London N1 2HY
Tel: 020 7359 2244   Fax: 020 7359 1616
email: mail@mqpublications.com

Text © David Baird 2002
Design concept: Broadbase
Design: Philippa Jarvis

ISBN: 1-84072-371-8

1 3 5 7 9 10 8 6 4 2

Printed and bound in China